HERBIVORES

Jill Foran

www.av2books.com

AV² provides enriched content that supplements and complements this book. Weigl's AV² books strive to create inspired learning and engage young minds in a total learning experience.

Your AV² Media Enhanced books come alive with...

 Audio
Listen to sections of the book read aloud.

 Key Words
Study vocabulary, and complete a matching word activity.

 Video
Watch informative video clips.

 Quizzes
Test your knowledge.

 Embedded Weblinks
Gain additional information for research.

 Slide Show
View images and captions, and prepare a presentation.

 Try This!
Complete activities and hands-on experiments.

... and much, much more!

Go to **www.av2books.com**, and enter this book's unique code.

BOOK CODE

L336645

AV² by Weigl brings you media enhanced books that support active learning.

Published by AV² by Weigl
350 5th Avenue, 59th Floor
New York, NY 10118
Website: www.av2books.com   www.weigl.com

Library of Congress Cataloging-in-Publication Data

Foran, Jill.
 Herbivores / Jill Foran.
    p. cm. — (Food chains)
 Includes index.
 ISBN 978-1-61690-708-2 (hardcover : alk. paper) — ISBN 978-1-61690-714-3 (softcover: alk. paper)
 1. Herbivores—Juvenile literature. I. Title.
 QL756.5.F67 2011
 591.5'4—dc22   2010050997

Printed in the United States of America in North Mankato, Minnesota
3 4 5 6 7 8 9 0 15 14 13 12

122012
WEP031212

Project Coordinator Aaron Carr
Art Director Terry Paulhus

Photo Credits
Every reasonable effort has been made to trace ownership and to obtain permission to reprint copyright material. The publishers would be pleased to have any errors or omissions brought to their attention so that they may be corrected in subsequent printings.

Weigl acknowledges Getty Images as its primary image supplier for this title.

Contents

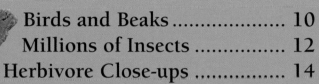

Nature's Food Chain

All living things need food to survive. Food provides the **energy** that plants and animals need to grow and thrive.

Plants and animals do not rely on the same types of food to live. Plants make their own food. They use energy from the Sun and water from the soil. Some animals eat plants. Others eat animals that have already eaten plants. In this way, all living things are connected to each other. These connections form food chains.

A food chain is made up of **producers** and **consumers**. Plants are the main producers in a food chain. This is because they make energy. This energy can be used by the rest of the living things on Earth. The other living things are called consumers.

There are five types of consumers in a food chain. They are carnivores, decomposers, herbivores, omnivores, and parasites. All of the world's organisms belong to one of these groups in the food chain.

Bees gather pollen from flowers as one of their food sources.

Chain Reactions

If an animal's food source disappears, other animals will suffer and possibly die.

FOOD CHAIN

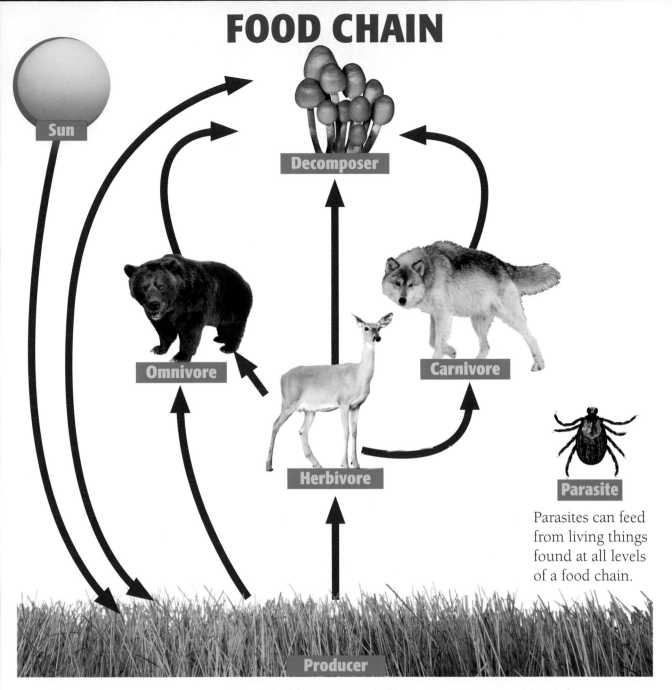

In this example, the Sun starts the food chain by providing energy for grass to grow. The deer eats grass as its food, and the wolf eats the deer. Bears may also eat grass or deer. Mushrooms receive energy from grass and the waste left behind by wolves, deer, and bears. Parasites can be found at any point along the food chain. They can live inside or on producers and consumers. A tick can get the food it needs to survive from a deer, a bear, or a wolf.

What Is a Herbivore?

Herbivore means "plant eater." It is a Latin word. The term herbivore describes animals in the food chain that eat only plants and **vegetation**. Herbivores get their energy from eating plant materials. This can include flowers, fruit, grasses, leaves, and even wood.

Herbivores are able to **digest** the plants they eat. Then, they convert the energy in the plant cells for their own use. Some examples of herbivores include deer, elephants, and rabbits. Most insects and many types of birds are also plant eaters.

Rabbits feed on a wide variety of vegetation, including grass and leaves.

The diets of herbivores vary. Some herbivores feed on only one type of plant. Others eat all kinds of vegetation. Many herbivores do not have to look hard for their food. For example, cows are usually surrounded by the grasses they need to eat in order to survive. Other herbivores must work harder to find food and survive.

Calves drink their mother's milk early in their lives before switching to eating grass and other vegetation.

In the world's **temperate** zones, herbivore diets depend on the season. This is because different plant foods grow during different times of the year. In the spring, herbivores might eat the tender shoots or growths of blooming plants. In the winter, they might eat the bark of bare trees.

Picky Eaters

Herbivores that eat only one kind of plant are called monophagous. The koala is a monophagous herbivore. It eats only eucalyptus tree leaves.

Built for Plant-eating

All herbivores have features that are **adapted** to their diets. Many herbivores have special body parts that help them chew and digest plant material.

Among the most important body features of all herbivores are their teeth. These teeth are designed for eating vegetation.

Herbivores that gnaw on plants have sharp **incisors** for cutting through nuts, wood, and other thick plant material. Herbivores that grind their food before swallowing, such as caribou, elk, or other kinds of deer, have flat **molars** for grinding their meals.

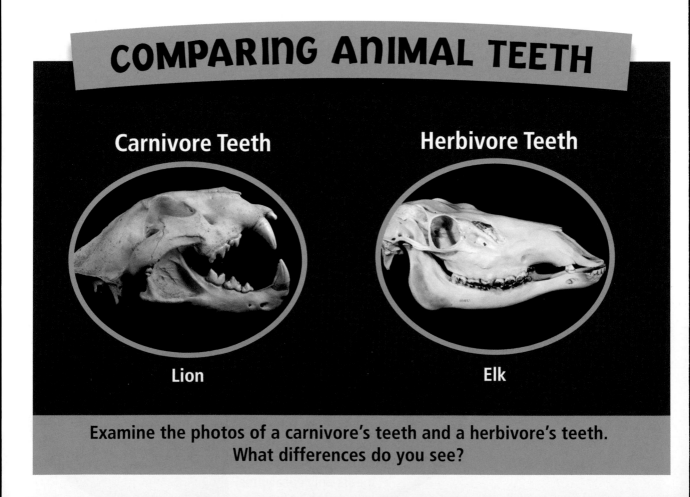

COMPARING ANIMAL TEETH

Carnivore Teeth

Lion

Herbivore Teeth

Elk

Examine the photos of a carnivore's teeth and a herbivore's teeth.
What differences do you see?

Cows have four chambers in their stomach instead of just one. When a cow swallows grass or other plants, the food goes to the first chamber, called the rumen. There, **bacteria** break down the food into something called cud. Later, when the cow is resting, it brings the cud back to the mouth and chews it again. The cud is then swallowed and passes through the other three stomach chambers. This process makes digestion easier.

Other herbivores with similar stomachs include antelope, bison, deer, and sheep. Mammals with more than one stomach chamber are called **ruminants**.

Bison usually eat during the day. Their diet consists of grass, leaves, twigs, and bark from a variety of bushes.

Jaws

The jaws of many herbivore mammals move from side to side instead of up and down. This helps these animals grind and crush tough plant material.

Birds and Beaks

Many kinds of birds are herbivores. Herbivorous birds do not have teeth. Instead, they use their beaks to eat. Some birds, such as the hawfinch and the parrot, use their short, strong beaks to open nuts and seeds. Their beaks act much the same way that a nutcracker works.

Sapsuckers do not crack nuts with their beaks. These birds eat the sugary sap out of trees. They use their long, sharp beaks to dig holes in trees and draw the sap out.

Parrots have strong feet with two toes in front and two in back. Their feet help them climb and grasp branches while they eat the fruits and seeds of trees.

Another type of herbivorous bird is the hummingbird. This tiny bird drinks the sugary **nectar** found deep inside flowers.

When a hummingbird is eating a meal, it uses its beak, tongue, and wings. It pokes its long, thin beak into a flower and stretches out its tongue. The tongue acts like a straw and sucks the liquid out of the flower. As the hummingbird drinks, it hovers over the flower by flapping its wings very quickly. Hummingbirds are the only birds that can fly backward and sideways, as well as forward.

A hummingbird's feet are too weak to support its weight on flat surfaces. The bird must hover over a flower when it is feeding.

Crushing Food

Most birds have a special muscular portion of their stomach called a gizzard. The gizzard helps birds to digest food. It crushes and grinds grains, hard nuts, and seeds. Some birds may also swallow small stones and gravel. This can help the gizzard grind and crush.

Millions of Insects

Many kinds of insects eat only plants. In fact, insects make up the largest number of herbivores. There are more insects in the world than all other forms of life put together. Scientists have identified more than 1 million insect **species**. Some scientists think there are millions more insect species that have not yet been discovered. Many species of beetles, flies, grasshoppers, moths, and snails are plant eaters.

Large swarms of migratory grasshoppers, including locusts, feed on crops, such as barley, corn, oats, rye, and wheat. These insects take only a few hours to damage an area.

One of the most beautiful insect herbivores is the butterfly. Many species of butterfly are found around the world. Most butterflies thrive in **tropical** regions. They feed on nectar from flowers. They also drink the sweet juice from ripe fruits.

A butterfly uses its tubelike tongue to sip its meals. This tongue is called a proboscis. A butterfly unfolds the proboscis to sip nectar. When the butterfly finishes drinking, it rolls its proboscis underneath its head.

Some butterflies migrate to tropical regions for the winter. Flowers and fruits are more plentiful in these warmer places.

Big Changes

All butterflies start their lives as eggs. A butterfly usually lays its egg on a leaf. Soon, a caterpillar hatches from the egg. Later, the caterpillar will become a butterfly. As the caterpillar grows and changes, it eats. Some caterpillars will only eat the kind of plant on which they were born.

Herbivore Close-ups

There are many kinds of herbivores. They come in all shapes and sizes. Some of the world's largest and smallest animals are herbivores. Herbivores can be found in different parts of the world. Some herbivores live in bodies of water. Many of them live on land.

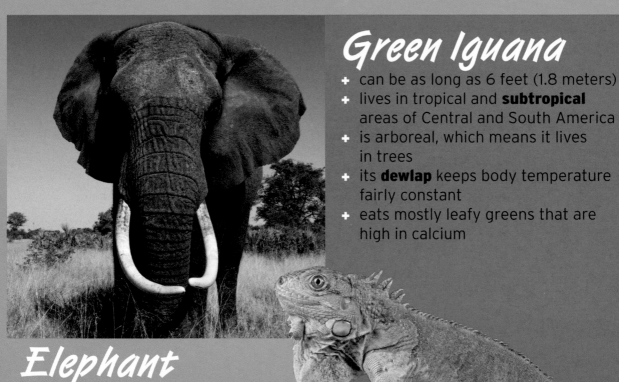

Green Iguana

+ can be as long as 6 feet (1.8 meters)
+ lives in tropical and **subtropical** areas of Central and South America
+ is arboreal, which means it lives in trees
+ its **dewlap** keeps body temperature fairly constant
+ eats mostly leafy greens that are high in calcium

Elephant

+ largest land mammal
+ lives in **savannah** grasslands and rainforests
+ muscular trunk picks up objects and rips branches from trees
+ tusks are incisor teeth, which keep growing throughout the animal's lifetime
+ eats bark, grasses, and leaves

Snail

+ most snails are herbivores
+ lives in fresh and salt water and in moist land areas
+ has a soft body protected by a hard shell, which it retreats into when threatened
+ the garden snail is the slowest-moving animal on Earth
+ eats living and decaying plants

Giraffe

+ tallest mammal; may be as tall as 18 feet (5.5 meters)
+ lives on the grassy plains of Africa
+ long neck enables it to eat from tall trees
+ can stretch its tongue more than 17 inches (43 centimeters) to get food
+ mostly eats the leaves and twigs of acacia trees

Manatee

+ is 10 feet (3 meters) long and weighs 1,200 pounds (545 kilograms); never stops growing
+ lives in fresh and salt water in Central, North, and South America
+ new teeth grow at the back of its mouth
+ eats more than 150 pounds (68 kilograms) of food each day
+ eats manatee and turtle grass, water hyacinth, and water lettuce

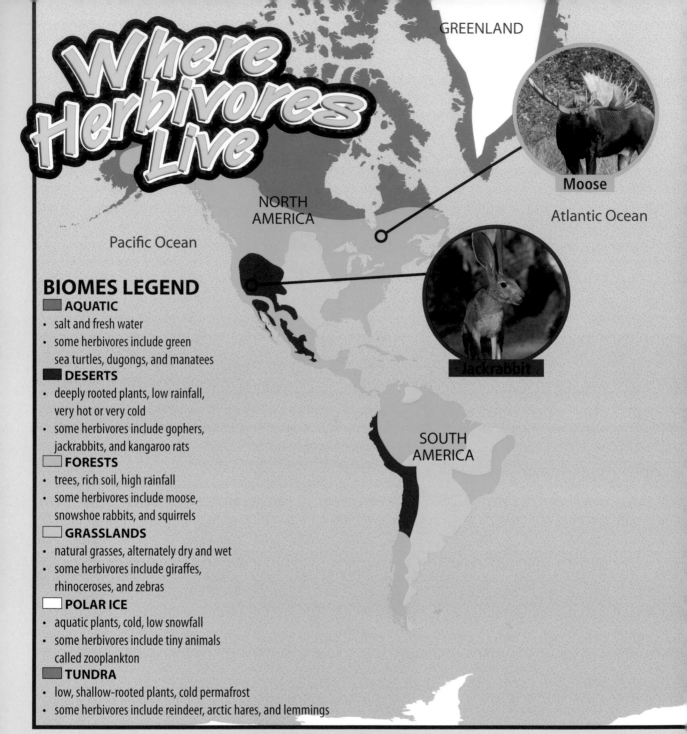

Where Herbivores Live

GREENLAND

Moose

NORTH
AMERICA

Pacific Ocean

Atlantic Ocean

Jackrabbit

SOUTH
AMERICA

BIOMES LEGEND

AQUATIC
- salt and fresh water
- some herbivores include green sea turtles, dugongs, and manatees

DESERTS
- deeply rooted plants, low rainfall, very hot or very cold
- some herbivores include gophers, jackrabbits, and kangaroo rats

FORESTS
- trees, rich soil, high rainfall
- some herbivores include moose, snowshoe rabbits, and squirrels

GRASSLANDS
- natural grasses, alternately dry and wet
- some herbivores include giraffes, rhinoceroses, and zebras

POLAR ICE
- aquatic plants, cold, low snowfall
- some herbivores include tiny animals called zooplankton

TUNDRA
- low, shallow-rooted plants, cold permafrost
- some herbivores include reindeer, arctic hares, and lemmings

All herbivores require special living conditions in order to thrive. The place where an animal lives is called its habitat. Earth has many different **biomes** that serve as habitats. Biomes are defined by their climates and by the plants and animals that live there. The world's largest biomes are aquatic, deserts, forests, grasslands, polar ice, and tundra.

A herbivore's habitat can be as big as a desert or a forest. It can also be as small as a tree branch or a pond. Each herbivore must live where it can get the food it needs to survive. Manatees live in the aquatic biome. They eat many types

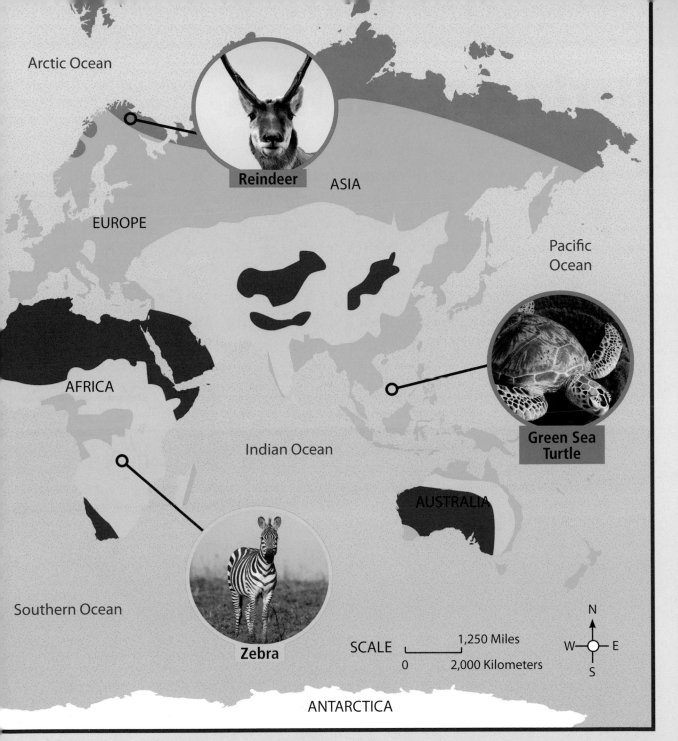

Arctic Ocean

Reindeer

ASIA

EUROPE

Pacific Ocean

AFRICA

Indian Ocean

Green Sea Turtle

AUSTRALIA

Southern Ocean

Zebra

SCALE |———————| 1,250 Miles
0   2,000 Kilometers

N
W ——○—— E
S

ANTARCTICA

of grasses and other plants that grow in water. They would not live long in deserts.

A herbivore that lives in a biome in one part of the world might not live in the same biome in a different part of the world. For example, giraffes live in the grasslands in Africa but not in the grasslands of North America.

Look at the map to see where some types of herbivores may live. Can you think of other herbivores? Where on the map do they live?

Herbivores at Risk

Plants and animals rely on each other in order to survive. For example, many birds and mammals eat the fruits that fall from forest trees. These animals then drop the seeds from the fruit. The seeds sprout into new plants. In this way, animals help to make new plants grow.

As bees collect pollen for food, they also spread it from flower to flower. Many plants cannot grow unless they are **cross-pollinated** by bees or other insects. If there were no flowers, bees would die. If there were no bees, many plant species would die.

In the United States in the 1980s, farmers rented bees from beekeepers to pollinate their crops. Pesticide use had greatly reduced the bee population.

The growth of new plants on cleared land occurs very slowly. It can take many years for the vegetation to grow back.

When a herbivore's habitat is destroyed and food is no longer available, that herbivore becomes **endangered**. Every day, herbivores ranging from insects to mammals become endangered or **extinct**. An endangered herbivore puts carnivores and plants at risk, too. In most cases, humans cause the world's plants and animals to become endangered. When people clear land to build communities or grow crops, many plants and animals lose their homes and their food supplies. Some environmental groups work to preserve the world's natural habitats.

The Karner blue butterfly is one of 400 endangered species of animals in the United States.

In The Field

PRIMATOLOGIST

Career
Primatologists study primates, such as gorillas and chimpanzees. Primatologists study a wide range of topics. This could include studying physical characteristics of primates and their ancestors, studying primates in their natural habitat, or studying their behavior.

Education
Most primatologists hold either a master's or a doctorate degree. Biology is usually a focus of study. Computer and writing skills are also important.

Working Conditions
Primatologists work in a range of environments. Some research primates in nature, while others conduct experiments in laboratories. Primatologists may also work at universities.

Tools
binoculars, camera, video camera, audio recorder, pencil, sketchbook, journal, maps, compass, global positioning system (GPS) device, computer, microscope.

Making an Energy Pyramid

A food chain is one way to chart the transfer of energy from one living thing to another. Another way to show how living things are connected is through an energy pyramid. An energy pyramid starts with the Sun. The Sun provides the energy that allows producers to grow. Producers are a source of energy for primary consumers in the next level of the pyramid. Primary consumers transfer energy up the pyramid to tertiary consumers. In this way, all living things depend on one another for survival. In the example below, grass is food for gazelles, and gazelles are food for lions.

ENERGY PYRAMID

Sun

Tertiary Consumers

Primary Consumers

Producers

Below are some examples of herbivores and the habitat where they live. Choose one of the animals and learn more about it. Using the Internet and your school library, find information about the animal's diet. Determine which plants the herbivore might eat. Using your herbivore as the primary consumer, draw an energy pyramid showing the transfer of energy. Which producers are a source of energy for the animal you picked? Which tertiary consumers receive energy from the primary consumer in your energy pyramid?

HERBIVORES

AQUATIC	Green Sea Turtle	Dugong	Manatee
DESERTS	Gopher	Jackrabbit	Kangaroo Rat
FORESTS	Moose	White-tailed Deer	Squirrel
GRASSLANDS	Giraffe	Rhinoceros	Elephant
TUNDRA	Caribou	Arctic Hare	Lemming

Quick Quiz

Based on what you have just read, try to answer the following questions correctly.

1. What does the word herbivore mean?

2. Where do giraffes live?

3. What is another name for a butterfly's tongue?

4. How many stomach chambers does a cow have?

5. What do hummingbirds eat?

6. Are plants considered producers or consumers in the food chain?

7. What is a monophagous herbivore?

8. What are an elephant's tusks?

adapted: changed over time to fit an environment

bacteria: one-celled living things too small for the human eye to see

biomes: large areas with the same climate and other natural conditions in which certain kinds of plants and animals live

consumers: animals that feed on plants or other animals

cross-pollinated: transfer of pollen from one flower to another

dewlap: the large flap of skin that hangs from a green iguana's throat

digest: to break down materials that can be used by the body

endangered: at risk of no longer living any place on Earth

energy: the usable power living things receive from food that they use to grow, move, and stay healthy

extinct: no longer living any place on Earth

incisors: front teeth used for cutting and gnawing

molars: large teeth used for grinding food

nectar: a sweet liquid found in many flowers

producers: living things, such as plants, that produce their own food

ruminants: animals that chew cud and have more than one stomach chamber

savannah: a flat plain covered with grass and a few trees

species: a group of the same kind of living things; members can breed together

subtropical: areas that are near and almost as warm as tropical areas

temperate: not too hot or too cold

tropical: areas that have a very warm climate year-round

vegetation: plant life

Log on to www.av2books.com

AV² by Weigl brings you media enhanced books that support active learning. Go to www.av2books.com, and enter the special code found on page 2 of this book. You will gain access to enriched and enhanced content that supplements and complements this book. Content includes video, audio, web links, quizzes, a slide show, and activities.

Audio
Listen to sections of the book read aloud.

Video
Watch informative video clips.

Embedded Weblinks
Gain additional information for research.

Try This!
Complete activities and hands-on experiments.

WHAT'S ONLINE?

Try This!	Embedded Weblinks	Video	EXTRA FEATURES
Test your knowledge of food chains.	Discover more herbivores.	Watch a video introduction to herbivores.	**Audio** Listen to sections of the book read aloud.
Outline the features of a herbivore.	Learn more about one of the herbivores in this book.	Watch a video about a herbivore.	
Research a herbivore.	Find out more about herbivore conservation efforts.		**Key Words** Study vocabulary, and complete a matching word activity.
Compare herbivores that live in different areas.	Learn more about herbivores.		
Try an interactive activity.			**Slide Show** View images and captions, and prepare a presentation.
			Quizzes Test your knowledge.

AV² was built to bridge the gap between print and digital. We encourage you to tell us what you like and what you want to see in the future.

Sign up to be an AV² Ambassador at www.av2books.com/ambassador.